Original title:
Beneath the Dreamy Sky

Copyright © 2024 Creative Arts Management OÜ
All rights reserved.

Author: Lorenzo Barrett
ISBN HARDBACK: 978-9916-90-570-8
ISBN PAPERBACK: 978-9916-90-571-5

The Galaxies of Our Dreams

In twilight's hush, our visions soar,
Each star a wish, forevermore.
Across the sky, our secrets gleam,
A canvas vast—a cosmic dream.

We dance on clouds of silver light,
Beneath the moon, the world feels right.
Entwined in hopes, with hearts aglow,
In galaxies where lovers flow.

With every breath, we reach the skies,
As stardust whispers and time flies.
In gravity's pull, our souls are free,
Exploring realms of you and me.

In cosmic tides, we drift and glide,
Through nebulas where dreams reside.
The universe, a boundless scheme,
Awakes our hearts in endless dream.

Night's Embrace on Hollowed Ground

Beneath the stars, the shadows dance,
In moonlit glow, we find our chance.
With soft winds whispering our name,
In silence wrapped, we play the game.

The ancient trees hold stories deep,
Where echoes of the night still weep.
On hollowed ground, we lay our fears,
In darkened corners, love appears.

The chill of night brings gentle peace,
While dreams and fears collide, then cease.
With every heartbeat, time stands still,
In night's embrace, we find our will.

Together here, where spirits roam,
In the stillness, we feel at home.
As shadows fade with dawn's first light,
We rise anew, from endless night.

A Veil of Midnight Mysteries

In shadows deep, the whispers weave,
A tapestry of secrets, aggrieve.
Stars blink softly, a celestial sigh,
Guardians of stories that never die.

Moonlit paths through the darkened trees,
Rustling leaves echo ancient pleas.
Each flicker holds a tale untold,
Wrapped in a veil of midnight gold.

Journeying Through the Night's Heart

With every step, the night unfurls,
A world where time slows and twirls.
Dreams take flight on wings of gray,
Through starlit realms, we wistfully sway.

Footprints echo on cobblestone lanes,
Where laughter lingers and love remains.
In shadows' clasp, we find our way,
A journey bright, though skies turn gray.

Twilight's Embrace

As day surrenders to night's tender call,
Shadows stretch as the sun starts to fall.
Colors blend in a soft embrace,
Whispers linger, time slows its pace.

The horizon blushes, a gentle sigh,
While stars awaken in the velvet sky.
In this magic hour, hearts unite,
Beneath the glow of the fading light.

A Dance of Lumens

Dancing fireflies twinkle in flight,
Painting the darkness with shimmering light.
As they weave through the night's cool air,
A ballet of lumens, bold and rare.

Whispers of wonders, soft and bright,
Guide wandering souls through the quiet night.
In their glow, we find our song,
A dance of moments, where we belong.

Starlight Stories Unraveled

Beneath the sky, a tale unfolds,
Whispers of dreams, both shy and bold.
Stars weave secrets in the night,
Guiding hearts toward the light.

Each glimmer tells of hopes once lost,
A cosmic dance, no matter the cost.
Through shadows deep, we seek our way,
With starlit maps to save the day.

In every twinkle, a laughter shared,
The universe watches; we are cared.
Feel the magic, let it be known,
In starlight stories, we find our home.

So drift with me on this celestial sea,
Where constellations write our decree.
In the silence, the cosmos sways,
Eternal dreams through endless days.

Aurora's Soft Embrace

Morning whispers in hues so bright,
Auroras dance in the canvas of night.
Colors blending, a gentle kiss,
In nature's arms, we find our bliss.

With every hue, the heart takes flight,
Caressed by warmth, dispelling fright.
The sky ignites with a soothing glow,
In this embrace, we learn to let go.

Beneath this banner of light, we stand,
Unity formed, hand in hand.
Through shifting tides and subtle grace,
We find our peace in Aurora's embrace.

As dawn awakens the sleeping land,
Hope resonates in each soft strand.
In the quiet, the world aligns,
With every breath, our spirit shines.

Ephemeral Echoes in Indigo

In twilight's grip, shadows play,
Indigo dreams drift far away.
Each fleeting moment, a breath in time,
Resounds in echoes, soft and sublime.

Whispers linger in the evening air,
A tapestry woven with utmost care.
Each glance, a story, overgrown,
In the quiet, the heart is sewn.

As dusk descends, feelings ignite,
Stars appear, challenging the night.
Chasing shadows, we dance alone,
In these echoes, our souls are known.

The indigo sky cradles the light,
Guiding lost spirits to new heights.
In the silence, a truth we find,
Ephemeral echoes, forever entwined.

The Realm of Distant Reverie

Dreamers gather in the silent night,
In a realm where wishes take flight.
Clouds of thought softly align,
Painting visions, pure and divine.

In echoes of laughter, memories reside,
In this haven, fears subside.
Each heartbeat sings of tales untold,
In distant reverie, we grow bold.

Through the mist, we chase the stars,
Leaving behind our earthly scars.
In the embrace of endless skies,
The realm of dreams forever lies.

So let us wander, hand in hand,
Across this ethereal land.
In the whispers, our truths will gleam,
In the heart of night, we find our dream.

Whirls of Cosmic Wonder

Stars dance in the velvet sky,
Whispers of the galaxies sigh.
Planets twirl in the cosmic breeze,
Time floats gently, like leaves on trees.

Nebulae paint with colors bright,
Eternal shadows, a silent flight.
Comets streak with tails of flame,
In this vastness, we are but a name.

The Night's Secret Garden

Moonlight bathes the blooms in white,
Night's perfume drifts and takes flight.
Crickets hum a lullaby,
While dreams gather 'neath the sky.

Petals whisper as night's breeze sighs,
Hidden secrets beneath starlit eyes.
Wonders bloom in shadow's keep,
Cradling nothing but magic deep.

Floating Palaces of the Mind

Thoughts ascend on clouds of grace,
Mind's creations, a sacred space.
Castles rise from dreams of lore,
Carved by wishes, forevermore.

Winding paths through visions bright,
Guiding hearts toward endless light.
In these halls, we dance and glide,
Where our hopes and fears reside.

Lullabies of the Ether

Softly sung by stars so far,
Night's embrace, our guiding star.
Echoes of the universe's song,
Whispers where the dreams belong.

Shadows hum a gentle tune,
Cradled under the silver moon.
Each note drifts on a silky stream,
Gifting peace, like a tender dream.

A Dance with the Clouds

White waltzing forms in the sky,
Drifting slowly, floating high.
Whispers of a gentle breeze,
Nature's soft and calming tease.

Shadows cast as they sway low,
Chasing sunlight, sweet and slow.
Gathering storms then parting ways,
A fleeting dance of sunlit rays.

When Wishes Take Flight

Stars twinkle bright in the night,
Hopes arise with the first light.
Dreams unleashed on gentle wings,
Chasing joy that freedom brings.

With every breath, we let go fears,
Casting hopes like whispered cheers.
Across the sky, so vast and wide,
Our deepest wishes choose to glide.

Under a Tapestry of Dreams

Beneath the stars, a world unfolds,
A story whispered, secrets told.
Threads of silver, gold, and blue,
Woven hearts in night's embrace, too.

Softly glimmers, the moon's reply,
Painting visions across the sky.
In the silence, we find our way,
Under dreams where wishes stay.

The Horizon's Silken Embrace

Where the sky kisses the sea,
Limitless horizons call to me.
Colors dance in fading light,
A canvas painted, pure delight.

Waves whisper tales of lands unknown,
As weary hearts begin to roam.
In twilight's glow, we find our place,
In the horizon's silken embrace.

A Symphony of Stars

In the night where silence sings,
Whispers of the cosmos ring,
Each twinkling light a tale unfolds,
A symphony in hues of gold.

Galaxies swirl in a dance so grand,
Notes of wonder guide our hand,
Stardust dreams, we weave with grace,
In the vast and endless space.

Feel the pulse of the universe's beat,
As we glide on this ethereal street,
Every heartbeat aligns with fate,
A harmony we celebrate.

In shadows deep, our hopes ignite,
Turning darkness into light,
Together we find our way afar,
Lost in the symphony of stars.

Wanderlust in the Blue

Beneath the sky so vast and clear,
Waves of freedom draw us near,
With every breeze, adventure calls,
A journey awaits as twilight falls.

Across the shores where dreams abide,
We let the ocean be our guide,
Fleeting moments, treasures found,
As wanderlust in waves resound.

Seashells whisper secrets old,
Stories of the brave and bold,
With every tide, we chase the hue,
Forever lost in wanderlust's view.

Footprints traced in golden sand,
Memories weaved by nature's hand,
In the blue, our spirits soar,
Wanderlust forevermore.

The Charm of Starlight

In the hush of midnight's flame,
Whispers dance, calling your name,
Starlight drapes the world anew,
A charming glow, a bright debut.

Softly the moon weaves tales of love,
Guiding hearts from above,
Twinkling gems that softly weave,
A charm of magic we believe.

In every glimmer, hope ignites,
Promises bright as starry nights,
Lost in wonder, hearts take flight,
Under the spell of starlight bright.

Moments captured in silver beams,
As we wander through our dreams,
In the glow, there's peace aflow,
The charm of starlight's gentle glow.

Celestial Footprints

On the sands of cosmic time,
We leave our marks, a dance so prime,
Footprints tracing paths of fate,
A journey vast, it won't be late.

Stars above, a guiding hand,
Written tales upon the sand,
In the light, our spirits blend,
Celestial journeys never end.

Every step, a story told,
Moments cherished, brave and bold,
Through the galaxies, we glide,
In the universe, we confide.

With every dawn, the past we greet,
In the stardust, we find our beat,
Together we roam through night so bright,
Leaving behind our celestial light.

Moonbeams in a Bottle

Silver light trapped tight,
A dance of shadows bright,
Whispers of the night,
In glass, a pure delight.

Captured in a gleam,
Reality, a dream,
Mysteries that teem,
In moonlit's gentle beam.

A vessel of the stars,
Holding the night's memoirs,
With each soft, bright spar,
True wonder travels far.

When dawn breaks the spell,
The secret bids farewell,
Yet in hearts it dwells,
A quiet, magic well.

A Voyage Through the Aether

Sailing on a stream,
Where starlit visions dream,
Beyond the world's seam,
In cosmic twilight's beam.

Winds of time do blow,
Guiding where thoughts flow,
Chasing shadows slow,
In realms of ebb and flow.

Galaxies unfurl,
In silence, thoughts twirl,
Exploring every pearl,
In the vastness, we whirl.

Beneath the dark sea,
A journey wild and free,
Through ether's tapestry,
Our spirits dance in glee.

The Nightingale's Whimsy

Soft notes fill the air,
A tale beyond compare,
Through whispers, it dares,
To paint dreams rare and fair.

Feathers touched by night,
In shadows, pure delight,
The stars blink in sight,
As songs take their flight.

Each melody weaves,
A tapestry of leaves,
The heart gently grieves,
Yet joy it also leaves.

In twilight's last hue,
The world feels anew,
A nightingale's cue,
To love, forever true.

Cascading Dreams

Waterfalls of thought,
In twilight, gently caught,
Each vision, finely wrought,
In dreams that time forgot.

Rivers of the mind,
Secrets left behind,
In currents, intertwined,
A treasure few can find.

Whispers long and deep,
Through the silence, we leap,
Into the realms of sleep,
Where colorful shadows creep.

With dawn's first embrace,
We awaken to grace,
As dreams leave their trace,
In the light's warm face.

Starlit Pathways

Beneath the sky, soft whispers flow,
Twinkling lights in the night aglow.
A journey starts on silken ground,
Where dreams and wishes twirl around.

Footsteps trace in silvered dust,
Guided by the stars, we trust.
Each turn reveals a hidden tale,
In the hush where night winds sail.

Moonlit ribbons weave and dance,
Inviting hearts to take a chance.
In shadows deep, secrets await,
As starlit pathways illuminate fate.

Sojourn Through the Starlight

Glimmers flicker in the vast expanse,
A celestial fabric spins in a trance.
Footprints linger on the cosmic air,
Where dreams awaken, free from care.

Every star a wish, a silent prayer,
Tales of old echo, so rare.
We wander forth, hand in hand,
Through boundless realms of a twilight land.

Softly drift on the evening breeze,
In this embrace, we find our ease.
The night, a canvas rich and deep,
As starlight guides us into sleep.

A Tidal Wave of Night

Across the horizon, shadows play,
In a tide of twilight, dreams sway.
Each wave a story, each pulse a sigh,
Under the gaze of a watchful sky.

The ocean breathes with a gentle hum,
As starlit whispers call us to come.
Together we dance on the silver strand,
With the universe cupped in our hand.

Moonbeams shimmer on rolling tides,
In the embrace where magic resides.
A tidal wave, the night unfolds,
In the heart where freedom enfolds.

Celestial Drifters

We float like leaves on a cosmic breeze,
Unraveling tales of the galaxies.
With every pulse, the night ignites,
As celestial drifters chase the lights.

Stars like lanterns in endless flow,
Illuminating paths we yearn to know.
In the dance of time, we lose our way,
Yet find our truth in the starlit play.

Eternal wanderers, forever free,
Wrapped in the fabric of destiny.
In the quiet, we hear the call,
As celestial drifters embrace it all.

The Canvas of Stars

Ink spills from the night,
Painting dreams in the dark.
Whispered wishes take flight,
Twinkling like a spark.

Galaxies swirl above,
Soft glow in the cold air.
Each point a tale of love,
Hearts laden with prayer.

Moonlight drapes the earth,
A cloak of silver sheen.
Nature's quiet rebirth,
In a world serene.

Under the vast expanse,
We find peace from afar.
In the cosmic dance,
We're held by each star.

Ethereal Nocturne

Silhouettes reach for the sky,
While shadows cling to the ground.
Stars murmur soft lullabies,
In the night, dreams are found.

Gentle breeze through the trees,
Carrying whispers of night.
Through the dark, a sweet tease,
Twinkling eyes full of light.

Crickets sing in the hush,
Lifting spirits with their song.
In the velvet-soft rush,
Where hidden hearts belong.

Moments drift like the mist,
Clinging close to our souls.
In every breath, a twist,
Of wonder that consoles.

Secrets in the Dew

Morning breaks with a sigh,
Dewdrops glimmer on grass.
In silence, whispers fly,
Among the blades that pass.

Nature's gems softly glow,
Holding stories untold.
In each bead, secrets flow,
Soft mysteries unfold.

A spider's web shines bright,
Delicate threads intertwine.
In the tender first light,
Nature's beauty divine.

With each dawn's gentle rise,
New beginnings take flight.
Hidden truths in disguise,
Awake in morning light.

Glimmers of a Midnight Wish

In the hush of midnight,
Wishes ride on moonbeams.
Hearts whisper soft and light,
Dancing around our dreams.

Stars twinkle, sparks of hope,
Lighting paths yet to tread.
In this moment, we cope,
With the thoughts in our head.

Dreamers gather like mist,
In the cool of the night.
Each desire, a sweet twist,
In the embrace of light.

As the world drifts and sighs,
We hold our dreams close to heart.
Under the endless skies,
Every wish, a fresh start.

The Serenity of Starlight

In the quiet night, stars align,
Whispers of peace, a gentle sign.
Moonlit paths on dreams ignite,
Serenity blooms in soft twilight.

Glistening gems in deep blue skies,
Each a wish, where silence lies.
Breathe in the calm, let worries flee,
Starlit moments set our hearts free.

Flickering flames in the cool night air,
Time drifts slowly, without a care.
Wrapped in wonder, we lose our fight,
Cradled gently in the starlight.

Embers of hope in the vast unknown,
A tapestry woven, not just our own.
Together we shine, forever bright,
In harmony found, in starlit flight.

Dancing with Shadows

In the dusk where whispers play,
Shadows spin in a graceful sway.
Dancers twirl in soft disguise,
Fleeting forms beneath dark skies.

Silent echoes in the night,
Mysterious steps, a hidden light.
Each shadow knows a secret tale,
Woven dreams where heartbeats sail.

Waltzing softly with the breeze,
Embracing night, it brings us ease.
Together we sway, lost and found,
In the dance where dark is crowned.

With every flicker, shadows gleam,
Painting life, a midnight dream.
In the rhythm of time's sweet grace,
We find our joy, in shadowed embrace.

Luminescence in the Silence

In the stillness, light does glow,
Softly speaks what hearts may know.
Whispers linger in the air,
Silence blooms beyond compare.

Moments captured, pure and bright,
Illuming paths with gentle light.
Radiance found in quiet thought,
In the hush, our spirits caught.

Shimmering thoughts drift like lace,
Carried forth in time and space.
Here we linger, void of sound,
In the peace, we are unbound.

Stars may fade, yet here we stand,
In the light, we touch the land.
Luminescence guides our way,
In silence deep, we softly sway.

A Thousand Sacred Stars

A thousand stars in velvet night,
Each one whispers, pure delight.
Dreams alive in the cosmic sea,
Guiding hearts to where they're free.

Constellations in endless flow,
Mapping journeys we long to know.
In their glow, we find our place,
A tapestry of love and grace.

With every twinkle, wishes rise,
Beneath the dance of ancient skies.
Sacred stories, softly told,
In the warmth of starlight bold.

A thousand dreams ignite the dark,
Filling souls with hopeful spark.
Together we soar, hearts apart,
In a universe, woven to art.

Hushed Echoes of Night

Whispers float through the dark sky,
Stars blink gently, a soft sigh.
Moonlight dances on the brook,
Dreams are woven in each nook.

Shadows crawl as silence speaks,
In the calm, the heart seeks.
Night's embrace, a velvet cloak,
Wrapped in stillness, words unspoke.

Footsteps muffled on the grass,
Moments linger, seconds pass.
In this hour, all feels right,
Lost in hushed echoes of night.

The Veil Between Worlds

Softly shimmering, the thin divide,
Whispers echo from the other side.
Beneath the surface, stories swell,
Tales of longing, tales to tell.

Glimmers dance in twilight's glow,
Threads of fate begin to flow.
In the silence, we connect,
Bridging dreams we can't reject.

Every heartbeat, every sigh,
Casts a light in the twilight sky.
The veil thins, and truths unfurl,
Intertwined, our hidden world.

Driftwood in the Dreamscape

A driftwood piece on shores of thought,
Carried by tides, a lesson taught.
In the current, it gently sways,
Lost in memory's endless maze.

Beneath the surface, shadows play,
Echoes of dreams drift far away.
Time stands still as visions blend,
In the stillness, hearts can mend.

Each grain of sand a story spun,
Tales of moonlight, tales of sun.
Through the depths, we find our way,
Like driftwood in the dreamscape stray.

Mist on the Mountain's Edge

Fog rolls in on the mountain peak,
Nature whispers low and bleak.
Veil of mystery, soft and white,
Cloaks the world in gentle night.

Footsteps vanish in shrouded haze,
Lost in loops of nature's maze.
Time slows down; the heart can breathe,
In the mist, we dare to weave.

Each inhale, a story shared,
Of dreams and hopes, of hearts prepared.
On the edge, where silence sings,
We embrace what the mist brings.

Stars Between Fingers

Whispers of light in the dark,
I trace the sky with my hand.
Constellations dance, leave a mark,
Each twinkle, a story to understand.

Fingers entwining with dreams,
I reach for the vastness above.
In the silence, a soft moonbeams,
Woven in night, wrapped in love.

Galaxies swirl in my grasp,
Holding the cosmos so near.
Time itself seems to clasp,
Moments of wonder, crystal clear.

Restless night, where shadows play,
I find solace in cosmic sighs.
Stars guide my thoughts on their way,
Connecting with echoes of the skies.

Celestial Harmonies

Melodies drift on starlit winds,
Notes twinkle from afar.
In the silence, the universe spins,
Each chord a guiding star.

Whispers of planets align,
A symphony of the unknown.
Cosmic rhythms, so divine,
In harmony, we are grown.

Echoes of ages, soft and low,
Resonate in the night's embrace.
Celestial songs gently flow,
Uniting all in their grace.

As the night unfolds its wings,
All creation sways to the tune.
In this dance, each being sings,
Beneath the watching moon.

The Dream Weaver's Canvas

Threads of night in gentle hand,
Stitching stars with silver gleam.
Patterns form, a woven strand,
In the quiet, we weave a dream.

Colors blend in twilight's grace,
Each hue a whisper, soft and true.
Canvas stretched in timeless space,
Painting visions for me and you.

Fantastical realms begin to rise,
Mountains soar, rivers of light.
Invented worlds beneath our eyes,
Guided onward by the night.

Within this tapestry we dwell,
Stories born in dreams we cast.
In the silence, magic swells,
A universe, vast and unsurpassed.

The Stillness of the Night Chorus

Under the blanket of deep black,
The world holds its breath in peace.
Crickets chirp, a gentle track,
In the stillness, worries cease.

Moonlight wraps the earth so tight,
Luna's glow on sleeping trees.
Stars blink softly, lost in flight,
Guiding dreams upon the breeze.

Silence hangs like a sweet refrain,
Echoing through the velvet air.
In the calm, we share the same,
A moment savored, free from care.

As night whispers its softest song,
Hearts unite in quiet shows.
In this stillness, we belong,
Together in the night's soft throes.

A Canvas of Cosmic Colors

Stars sprinkle the velvet sky,
Whispers of colors drift by.
Nebulae dance in vibrant hues,
Painting dreams with cosmic views.

Galaxies spiral, swirling bright,
In the depths of endless night.
Each brushstroke a tale untold,
A universe in wonders bold.

Comets streak with fiery grace,
Tracing paths in this vast space.
In the silence, beauty sings,
As the cosmos unfolds its wings.

Floating on the Veil of Night

Drifting softly on the breeze,
Moonlight filters through the trees.
Whispers echo in the dark,
As the night ignites its spark.

Shadows dance upon the ground,
In the silence, peace is found.
Stars above twinkle so bright,
Floating gently on this night.

The world fades to a distant hum,
As dreams unfold, we start to come.
Floating freely, hearts take flight,
Lost in the veil of the night.

Serenade of the Moonlit Horizon

Silvery beams caress the sea,
As the waves sing soft and free.
The moon gazes down with pride,
A serenade of the tide.

Whispers of winds play along,
In this night where we belong.
With each pulse, the waters gleam,
Reflecting every dreamer's dream.

The horizon blurs in the glow,
Where the land and water flow.
In this moment, hearts combine,
Underneath the stars that shine.

Tranquil Reflections of the Cosmos

Quiet pools of endless night,
Mirroring the stars' soft light.
In calm waters, thoughts take flight,
Reflecting wonders, pure delight.

Stillness reigns in this embrace,
As the universe finds its place.
Ripples dance on surfaces wide,
Carrying secrets deep inside.

The cosmos whispers gentle truths,
Painting hope in life's own booths.
In tranquil moments, we can see,
The universe inside of me.

Radiance of the Dusk

In the sky, colors blend,
Orange and pink, a calming send.
Whispers of night draw near,
The day bids us all to clear.

Shadows dance on the ground,
As silence starts to surround.
Stars twinkle, shy at first,
Bringing dreams to quench our thirst.

A soft glow on the horizon,
Fading light, a sweet prison.
Nature's brush paints with ease,
In the air, a gentle breeze.

Evening's grace fills the heart,
From this peace, we shall not part.
Embrace the dusk's warm glow,
Let our spirits softly flow.

Under the Cosmic Embrace

Beneath the vast and endless sky,
Stars like diamonds linger high.
Galaxies swirl in cosmic dance,
Inviting hearts to take a chance.

Moonlight spills a silver hue,
Illuminating dreams anew.
Planets wink with gentle grace,
In this vast, enchanted space.

We lie down on the cool, soft grass,
Listening to the night hours pass.
The universe whispers its song,
To which every soul belongs.

Together we bask in the night,
Wrapped in the cosmos, pure delight.
In this moment, time stands still,
A perfect peace, our hearts to fill.

The Mirage of Dreams

In the twilight, shadows play,
Crafting visions that sway.
Waves of thought, like gentle streams,
Flowing softly through our dreams.

Mirages rise in the soft mist,
Whispers of hope we can't resist.
The heart dances, free and bright,
Chasing echoes of delight.

Each thought flickers, fades away,
Yet in silence, they remain.
A tapestry woven with care,
Fragile dreams floating in air.

As we drift through this realm untold,
Embrace the warmth, let dreams unfold.
In mirages, we find our way,
Guided by the light of day.

Serenade of the Night Breeze

Gentle whispers through the trees,
Carried softly on the breeze.
Songs of nature, pure and sweet,
A melody that stirs the feet.

Stars above, they nod in time,
To the rhythm, the perfect rhyme.
Crickets chirp, a backing choir,
In the night, our souls inspire.

Moonlit paths weave through our dreams,
Like silver threads in flowing streams.
Each sigh of night brings us near,
In this hush, all hearts adhere.

Let the breeze guide us along,
In this serenade, we belong.
Under starlight, we will sway,
Together, we dance till the day.

Dancing with Shadows in the Dark

In the stillness of night, we sway,
With shadows that flicker and play.
Whispers of silence take flight,
As we dance with the dreams of twilight.

Footsteps echo on the cold ground,
In the realm where the lost are found.
The moonlight wraps us in a shroud,
While shadows waltz, eloquent and proud.

Hearts entwined beneath the stars,
Each glance an unspoken memoir.
The night holds secrets, softly spun,
In the dance of shadows, we are one.

With every twirl, the darkness sings,
A melody borne from ancient springs.
In the realm where the stillness throngs,
We'll dance all night to the shadows' songs.

Celestial Dreams Whispered in Twilight

As dusk descends with a gentle sigh,
Dreams of stardust paint the sky.
Softly the whispers of night arise,
Caressing the world with silent ties.

In the cradle of twilight's embrace,
Celestial wonders find their place.
The horizon glimmers, a soft caress,
In the twilight, we find our guess.

Fading light kisses the day goodbye,
In this moment, the heart learns to fly.
Stars awaken, their stories unfold,
In celestial dreams, the universe told.

A tapestry woven of twilight's breath,
Where hopes take flight and fears find death.
In this quiet hour, all hearts collide,
Celestial dreams, our eternal guide.

Whispers of the Celestial Veil

Beneath the vastness of the night,
Whispers dance in ethereal light.
The stars weave tales with gentle grace,
In the embrace of the cosmic space.

Veils of mystery flutter and sway,
Guiding souls who've lost their way.
Each whisper beckons with a soft charm,
Lifting spirits high, keeping them warm.

In the hush of the galaxy's sigh,
Time stands still, as dreams float by.
Celestial secrets call to the brave,
In whispers soft, our souls they save.

Through the chasms of the swirling skies,
Hope ignites in the heart that tries.
With every twinkle and every veil,
We chase the whispers that softly prevail.

Starlit Reverie

In the quiet of night, dreams take flight,
Beneath the canopy of stars so bright.
Whispers of hope in the velvet air,
Cradle our thoughts with tender care.

Glistening starlight, a pathway formed,
In the heart's embrace, we are warmed.
Each flicker a promise, each glow a chance,
In this starlit ocean, we find our dance.

Time drips slowly like honey new,
Wrapped in the glow of the shimmering view.
The universe pulses, alive and real,
In the starlit reverie, our hearts we seal.

As night unfolds in its wondrous hue,
We dream the dreams meant for me and you.
In every heartbeat, every sigh,
Starlit moments will never die.

Secrets from a Silvered Sky

Beneath the veil of stars so bright,
Whispers of dreams take silent flight.
In the hush of night, they softly sigh,
Guarding secrets from a silvered sky.

Echoes of wishes dance and spin,
Carried on the breeze, they begin.
Hidden tales in the dark unfold,
In shimmering light, their truths are told.

Glimmers of hope in the midnight air,
Sparkling tales of love and care.
The universe hums a timeless tune,
Beneath the watchful glow of the moon.

Through the darkness, a light shines near,
With every heartbeat, wisdom clear.
The night sky holds what hearts desire,
In its embrace, dreams rise and aspire.

The Wisp of a Shooting Star

A fleeting glimpse in the night's embrace,
A wisp of light, a moment's grace.
Across the heavens, swift it goes,
Leaving behind a trail that glows.

Eyes wide open, hearts in awe,
In a single breath, we feel the draw.
A wish is made, a promise cast,
In the spark of magic, dreams hold fast.

Speeding through dark, it dances free,
An echo of hope for you and me.
Transcending time in brilliant flight,
It holds our dreams in twinkling light.

When darkness falls, and silence reigns,
We search for signs, despite the chains.
With every wish upon a star,
We chase the wisps, no matter how far.

Celestial Echoes

In the vast expanse where starlight gleams,
Celestial echoes weave through dreams.
Timeless whispers from the deep,
Secrets of the night, savored and steeped.

Galaxies swirl in a cosmic dance,
Each twinkling light a chance, a chance.
To touch the infinite, hold it near,
And hear the universe crystal clear.

Comets race through the endless blue,
Marking paths where wishes renew.
With every pulse, the heavens sigh,
Painting stories against the sky.

In the silence, a symphony plays,
Of hope and love, in myriad ways.
Through the ages, echoes persist,
In the heart of night, we coexist.

Moonlit Whispers of Time

Under the watchful eye of the moon,
Time unfolds its gentle tune.
Soft whispers glide through the night,
Tracing shadows in silver light.

Moments linger, sweet and clear,
Each heartbeat a treasure we hold dear.
In the glow, memories dance and play,
Guiding us through the night and day.

Beneath the stars, our stories blend,
In moonlit dreams, we transcend.
The tapestry of moments, rich and divine,
Woven together in the fabric of time.

So let us listen, as the night unfolds,
To the whispers of time, as life molds.
In the moon's embrace, we find our way,
Through memories cherished, come what may.

Whispers in the Cosmic Breeze

In the depths where shadows play,
Gentle winds weave tales of day.
Stars twinkle softly, secrets shared,
In silken threads, the night is bared.

Galaxies dance in silent grace,
Each whisper reached from distant place.
Echoes of dreams, in silence bloom,
Carried softly through the loom.

Murmurs of light across the sky,
While cosmic hearts begin to sigh.
With every pulse, the universe sings,
Embracing all that wonder brings.

In these whispers, time stands still,
The cosmos breathes, a tranquil thrill.
Hold your breath, let your spirit soar,
In the breeze that knows so much more.

Garden of Stars and Longing

In a garden where the night's adorned,
Stars bloom like flowers, brightly scorned.
Petals of light, with dreams entwined,
Echoing wishes, lost but kind.

Moonbeams brush against the leaves,
In this haven, a heart believes.
Every twinkle holds a sigh,
A whispered prayer to the night sky.

Beneath the glow, desires ignite,
In shadows cast by soft starlight.
Each glimmer tells a story dear,
Of hopes that linger, ever near.

In this garden, a soft embrace,
Where every star finds its place.
Longing whispers through the air,
A tapestry of love laid bare.

When Daydreams and Nightfall Meet

In twilight's hush, a magic stirs,
Where daydreams linger, softly blurs.
Shadows blend with softening light,
In this dance, hearts take flight.

The horizon paints a tale so bright,
As day bows down to the coming night.
Stars tease the sky with their gentle gleam,
In this moment, we chase a dream.

Time holds its breath in quiet delight,
When day meets dusk, and wrong turns right.
Whispers of hope in colors unfurl,
As daydreams drift in a swirling whirl.

In every heartbeat, the world aligns,
Caught between borders of midnight signs.
Embrace the magic, let it flow,
As nightfall uncovers what dreams bestow.

Tides of Light on the Edge of Forever

On the brink where shadows lie,
Tides of light begin to cry.
In whispers soft, they beckon near,
Songs of hope for hearts to hear.

Each wave that breaks against the shore,
Carries tales of something more.
Dreams are woven in silver threads,
Where moonlit paths and starlight spreads.

Journey forth where shadows wane,
In the light, there's no more pain.
For every heart that dares to gleam,
Rides the waves of endless dreams.

On this edge, forever calls,
With open arms, the darkness falls.
In the tides, find your way true,
Let the light inspire you anew.

Twilight's Gentle Serenade

The sun dips low, a fiery glow,
As whispers dance in twilight's air.
Shadows stretch, their stories flow,
In this soft hum, we find our care.

Stars blink awake, a tranquil sight,
Night wraps us in its velvet fold.
Moonbeams cast a silver light,
In secret tales, the heart is bold.

Crickets sing in harmony,
Their music weaves through gentle night.
Nature's tune, a symphony,
In dream's embrace, we take our flight.

So let the evening softly sway,
As dreams arise, and spirits flee.
In twilight's arms, we'll gently stay,
Forever lost in reverie.

Floating on Slumber's Wings

A feathered touch, the night descends,
On whispers soft, it calls our name.
In dreams we sail, where time transcends,
As stardust breathes a silent flame.

The world below begins to fade,
With every sigh, we drift away.
In tranquil waves, our worries wade,
While moonlit beams in silence play.

A canvas vast, where visions bloom,
Through galaxies, we weave and spin.
In gentle peace, there's room for gloom,
Yet joy and hope draw us back in.

So float anew on slumber's wings,
Embrace the night, let go, be free.
In dreams reside, where magic clings,
A sweeter life is meant to be.

Celestial Stories Untold

In cosmic realms where starlight spills,
Ancient tales in silence bloom.
Each twinkling star with secrets fills,
A whisper washed in night's perfume.

Planets waltz in a dazzling trance,
As comets trace their fiery tails.
In darkness deep, they take their chance,
To share the truths that time unveils.

Galaxies swirl in a timeless dance,
As dreams and visions intertwine.
The universe calls, a beckoning glance,
In every heart, its stories shine.

So look above, let wonder soar,
In constellations, life's lore sings.
For in the night, forevermore,
Our souls unlock the cosmic rings.

Dreams Adrift on the Breeze

Upon the wind, our hopes take flight,
Like whispers soft through fields of gold.
They drift along, in sweet delight,
With every gust, new tales unfold.

A gentle breeze, a calming touch,
It sweeps us close, beneath the trees.
In nature's breath, we find so much,
As dreams dance wildly in the leaves.

The world a canvas, vast and wide,
Where colors blend in soft embrace.
With every heartbeat, side by side,
We chase the light, the fleeting grace.

So let us float on dreams adrift,
In harmony with time and space.
As whispers fade, we find our gift,
In every moment, love's sweet trace.

Whispers of Celestial Waves

The moonlight dances on the sea,
Soft whispers travel endlessly.
Stars twinkle in the silent night,
Guiding lost dreams to take flight.

Waves embrace the sandy shore,
Secrets held forevermore.
In the breeze, a song is sung,
Of ancient tales, forever young.

Celestial winds in gentle sway,
Carrying hearts that drift away.
Beneath the vast and endless skies,
Hope takes wing, and longing flies.

Each ripple holds a story true,
Whispers of love, both old and new.
In this quiet, sacred place,
Life's mysteries find their grace.

Chasing Stardust in Twilight

As the sun dips low, colors blend,
The day whispers its soft good end.
Stars awaken, one by one,
In the canvas where dreams are spun.

Fading light reveals the night,
Chasing stardust, feeling light.
Hearts collide in the dusk's embrace,
Moments captured, time's sweet chase.

Underneath the velvet dome,
We wander far, we feel at home.
Each twinkle calls, a siren's plea,
To follow paths where we are free.

In twilight's glow, we share a glance,
Caught in the magic of this dance.
As shadows merge with starlit beams,
We chase the threads of fleeting dreams.

The Lullaby of Evening Stars

The evening hums a soft refrain,
With twinkling stars that kiss the plain.
Moonbeams light the sleepy ground,
In the stillness, peace is found.

A lullaby weaves through the air,
Whispered secrets, sweet and rare.
Crickets sing their nightly tune,
As dreams awaken 'neath the moon.

Each star a note in night's soft song,
Filling hearts where dreams belong.
In this moment, all is right,
Wrapped in love, embraced by night.

So close your eyes, embrace the calm,
Let the universe be your balm.
For in its arms, you shall discover,
The lullaby of stars, a mother.

Echoes of a Midnight Caress

In the stillness, shadows play,
Midnight whispers drift away.
A caress from the night so deep,
Awakening dreams from slumber's keep.

Soft sighs of wind through trees entwine,
Echoing secrets, divine design.
Stars serve as witnesses, aglow,
To the heart's soft call, gentle and slow.

Every blink of light, a lover's glance,
In this moment, souls dance.
A symphony of night unfolds,
Wrapped in warmth, as time molds.

With each heartbeat, shadows glide,
Whispers of love we cannot hide.
In the embrace of night's sweet spell,
Echoes linger, a memory to tell.

Secrets Spun from Celestial Threads

In whispers soft, the stars declare,
Their hidden truths in midnight air.
With every twinkle, secrets weave,
A tapestry we dare believe.

Galaxies stretch, a boundless glance,
In twilight's hold, we find our chance.
To glimpse the worlds beyond our sight,
And dance with shadows in the night.

The cosmos hums a silent song,
Where ancient tales of love belong.
Each comet's tail, a fleeting sign,
Of mysteries in the grand design.

So let us gaze and ponder deep,
The promises that heavens keep.
For in this vast and starry dome,
We find our hearts, we find our home.

Dreams Adrift in Stellar Seas

Beneath the veil of midnight's sigh,
Dreams drift like ships in a starry sky.
With every wave, our hopes take flight,
On celestial tides of shimmering light.

The moonlight guides the wayward thoughts,
Through cosmic realms where time is caught.
Each twinkle sparks a wish anew,
In the deep blue, our spirits flew.

Galactic winds carry tales untold,
Of journeys vast and adventures bold.
With every heartbeat, the dreams ignite,
In stellar seas that greet the night.

Awake in slumber, we sail afar,
To galaxies kissed by a shooting star.
In dreams adrift, we are set free,
In the endless dance of infinity.

Variegated Clouds of Belief

In skies painted with colors bright,
Float clouds of hope in morning light.
Each shade a story, broad and vast,
Of dreams and wishes meant to last.

Beneath the arch of heavens wide,
Our hearts find refuge, dreams abide.
With every hue, we're intertwined,
In variegated paths we find.

Mornings whisper with gentle grace,
As sunlight warms a tender place.
Where clouds of belief drift and sway,
In the embrace of a brand-new day.

So let us cherish every hue,
The vibrant shades that shine so true.
In the gallery of our minds,
Variegated clouds, our hearts remind.

Twilight's Kiss on Distant Shores

When twilight falls on distant lands,
A gentle kiss from starlit hands.
With colors blended, day departs,
And whispers softly touch our hearts.

The ocean sighs a lullaby,
As waves embrace the twilight sky.
With every crest, a story told,
Of dreams and wishes, young and old.

The horizon glows in dusky light,
Where day and night in fusion unite.
In every flicker, hope takes wing,
In twilight's arms, our spirits sing.

So let us wander, hand in hand,
On shores where twilight softly stands.
In the embrace of dusk's caress,
We find our peace, we feel our bless.

Nightfall's Illuminated Path

Stars awaken in the sky,
Glowing softly, they draw nigh.
Whispers of the moonlit night,
Guide us with their silvery light.

Shadows dance upon the ground,
In the stillness, peace is found.
Each step taken, a gentle sigh,
Embracing darkness, we learn to fly.

The forest breaths, a hidden spark,
Echoes linger as we embark.
With every twinkle, tales unfold,
Of ancient secrets waiting to be told.

So let us wander, hand in hand,
Through night's embrace, across the land.
For every star, a dream's decree,
In nightfall's glow, we will be free.

Threads of Night's Fabric

Woven deep in twilight's seam,
Threads of silver softly gleam.
Stars entangled, a cosmic weave,
In the fabric that we believe.

Whispers from the starlit skies,
Telling tales where memory lies.
Glimmers spark in silence bold,
Fractals of the night unfold.

Sewing dreams with threads of light,
Binding hearts in gentle flight.
With each heartbeat, stories twine,
Through the darkness, hope will shine.

In this tapestry of night,
We find solace, pure delight.
For in each thread, the essence shows,
That in the dark, true magic grows.

Cosmic Currents

Rivers of stars flow far and wide,
In cosmic seas, we take a ride.
Planets swirl in a celestial dance,
Bound by gravity, lost in trance.

Comets blaze through velvet skies,
Traces left to mesmerize.
In every spark, a story waits,
Of countless worlds and their fates.

Galaxies spin in timeless grace,
Expanding through the vastness of space.
An endless journey, we embrace,
Riding currents, we find our place.

So lift your gaze and feel the flow,
As cosmic winds begin to blow.
For in the dark, we find our light,
Chasing dreams through the endless night.

The Lanterns of Dreams

Flickering lights in the evening haze,
Lanterns aglow, a guiding blaze.
Whispers of hope, they softly call,
Illuminating shadows that fall.

Each lantern holds a wish inside,
A flicker of faith, a heart open wide.
In the darkest hour, they brightly beam,
Casting warmth on the edges of dream.

So carry your lantern along the way,
Through storms of night, until break of day.
For dreams take flight on the wings of light,
As lanterns guide us through the night.

In every flicker, a promise lies,
The heart remembers, the soul will rise.
Together we journey, hand in hand,
Our dreams illuminated, a radiant band.

Nightfall's Embrace

As daylight fades, the shadows creep,
The stars awaken from their sleep.
A gentle hush, the world stands still,
In night's embrace, a soft thrill.

Whispers dance on the cool night air,
Secrets linger everywhere.
The moon ascends, a silver guide,
Through realms of darkness, we shall glide.

Softly now, the dreams take flight,
In the cradle of the quiet night.
The heartbeat of the earth grows slow,
In nightfall's arms, we ebb and flow.

With every star, a story told,
Of love and fears, and nights of old.
In the twilight's glow, we find our place,
Wrapped in the magic of nightfall's grace.

Moonlit Musings

Beneath the moon, my thoughts take flight,
In the stillness of the night.
A silver glow on whispered streams,
Awakens all my hidden dreams.

The clouds drift softly, veiling light,
Concealing wonders from my sight.
Yet in the dark, my heart can see,
The beauty of what's meant to be.

Each flicker in the sky above,
A reminder of the stars we love.
In shadows deep, my spirit roams,
Finding peace in these moonlit homes.

The night unfolds, a mystic page,
Where silence speaks in every stage.
With every sigh, I feel the call,
In moonlit musings, I find it all.

Echoes of a Cosmic Dream

In the depths of space, where starlight swirls,
Lie the dreams of boys and girls.
Echoes whisper across the night,
Telling tales of distant light.

Galaxies spin in silent grace,
Time entwined in endless space.
A cosmic dance of fate and chance,
Invites the heart to dream and prance.

Nebulas bloom like twilight flowers,
In their glow, we find our powers.
Through the vastness, we search and yearn,
For the wisdom in the stars to learn.

Each twinkling point, a story told,
Of ancient truths and futures bold.
In the dreamscape of the universe wide,
We find our place, in the stellar tide.

Fantasies in the Twilight

Glimmers of dusk in fading light,
Paint the sky with hues so bright.
As day gives way to night's embrace,
We wander through a mystic space.

Each shadow cast tells tales of old,
In twilight's warmth, the dreams unfold.
Fantasies take shape and form,
Within the dusk, a gentle storm.

The horizon glows, a fiery brand,
Inviting us to take a stand.
In whispers soft, the night winds sigh,
As shooting stars dash through the sky.

Embrace the quiet, feel the calm,
Let twilight wrap you in its charm.
With every breath, let worries cease,
In the fantasies of night, we find our peace.

Whispers Among the Constellations

In the silence of the night, we gaze,
Stars above in a silver haze.
Each twinkle tells a tale untold,
Whispers of dreams in the cosmos bold.

From Orion's belt to the Southern Cross,
Stories linger, no matter the loss.
Galaxies dance in ethereal light,
Guiding our hearts through the velvety night.

Celestial echoes, secrets unfold,
In the vastness, we feel consoled.
Nebulas painting the canvas above,
A tapestry woven with wonder and love.

Among the constellations, we find our way,
With hope and wonder, come what may.
In each whisper, a world waits to bloom,
As stardust dances in the night's gloom.

Fables of the Moonlit Shore

Beneath the moon's gentle silver light,
Waves whisper secrets throughout the night.
Shells scatter stories on soft, warm sand,
Fables carried by tides, as if planned.

The ocean beckons, a siren's call,
With each rising wave, we hear it all.
A tune of ages, of lost mariners,
Tales of adventure, of dreams and fears.

Footprints fade where the waters embrace,
Leaving behind a shimmering trace.
In the glow of the night, we find our lore,
Every heartbeat is a fable of the shore.

Together we sing, as the stars align,
Crafting our stories, your heart with mine.
In the end, it's love that we adore,
As the moon whispers fables forevermore.

The Tides of Reverie

In whispered dreams, the tides roll in,
Caressing shores where our tales begin.
Each wave a memory, ebbing and flow,
Lost in the depths where the wild dreams grow.

Beneath the surface, a world unseen,
Holds the echoes of what might have been.
The salty air carries hopes anew,
As the horizon blushes in twilight's hue.

With every heartbeat, a secret is spun,
Crafting a journey not easily done.
The sands shift gently, time stands still,
In the dance of the tides, we find our thrill.

Through the labyrinth of shadows and light,
Finding ourselves in the embrace of night.
Let the tides of reverie guide our way,
As dreams intertwine and softly sway.

Kaleidoscope of Twilight

As the sun dips low, colors collide,
In a kaleidoscope where dreams reside.
Hues of purple, orange, and gold,
A canvas of memories waiting to unfold.

Whispers of dusk in the cooling air,
Entwined with stars that begin to glare.
In the twilight's embrace, we breathe anew,
Every fleeting moment a vibrant view.

Echoes of laughter dance on the breeze,
Carried on whispers of rustling leaves.
In every shadow, there's magic to see,
A tapestry woven with life's mystery.

As darkness descends, the colors remain,
In the heart's canvas, they linger and stain.
Forever we hold the twilight's delight,
In the kaleidoscope of the approaching night.

A Driftwood Journey to Nowhere

Driftwood floats on waters deep,
Carried by currents, secrets keep.
Whispers of tides, tales untold,
In the vast expanse, you unfold.

A journey unfolds without a plan,
Through wild waves, where dreams began.
Lost and found in the ocean's sway,
A wanderer's heart, drifting away.

Each wave a story, each splash a cry,
Echoes of places where thoughts lie.
Bound to the sea, yet nothing finite,
Driftwood journeys into the night.

In the embrace of the moon's soft glow,
A path unknown, where lost things go.
Through tempests and calms, I will roam,
The driftwood journey, my heart's true home.

The Enigma of Endless Night

Under a sky of velvet black,
Stars like lanterns, light the track.
Cosmic whispers fill the air,
A riddle spoken, sweet and rare.

Shadows dance in the moonlit gloom,
Mysteries thrum like an ancient tune.
Eternal night holds secrets tight,
The enigma lingers, hidden in sight.

Dreams weave like silk in the stillness,
Silent echoes stitch the chillness.
Eyes gazing upwards, hearts alight,
We search for answers in endless night.

Through the darkness, a spark ignites,
Hope flickers softly, a guide in sights.
Embrace the mystery, let it flow,
For in endless night, we truly grow.

Soft Murmurs of the Galaxy

Whispers of stardust fill the void,
In cosmic swirls, our dreams enjoyed.
Nebulae blush with colors bright,
Soft murmurs echo through the night.

Galaxies spin in a gentle grace,
Each twirl a journey, a timeless race.
Infinite wonders beckon and call,
As we drift through the celestial hall.

Crickets sing on the ground below,
While the cosmos hums, serene and slow.
Together we dance to the stellar song,
Soft murmurs of galaxies, where we belong.

In the quiet of space, we find our peace,
A tapestry woven, never to cease.
Embracing the magic of the night sky,
Soft murmurs of the universe, sweet lullaby.

Threads of Solitude in the Cosmos

In the expanse where silence reigns,
Threads of solitude weave through pains.
Stars flicker softly, alone yet bright,
A tapestry spun in the vast night.

Each thread a whisper, a story unknown,
Stitched together, though far from home.
In this galaxy, we find a call,
Threads of solitude bind us all.

Galaxies swirl like thoughts in flight,
In solitude's embrace, we find our light.
Through the fabric of space, hearts align,
Threads of existence, yours and mine.

In the cosmic weave of time and space,
We are threads of solitude, each with grace.
Connected by stars, in the night's flow,
In the quiet cosmos, love will grow.

The Quiet Dance of Nightfall

The stars begin to twinkle bright,
As shadows stretch and take their flight.
Whispers of the night fill the air,
In gentle stillness, moments rare.

Silver moonlight bathes the ground,
A serene silence all around.
Crickets sing their lullaby,
While dreams awaken, take to sky.

Trees sway softly in the breeze,
Nature hums a lull with ease.
Each heartbeat drifts on night's embrace,
Lost in time, in slow-paced grace.

The world retreats, a tender sigh,
As night unfurls its velvet sky.
In this stillness, hearts may find,
The peace their souls have longed to bind.

Painted Visions from Above

Clouds brush strokes on canvas wide,
A palette swirling, dreams abide.
Sunset bleeds in crimson hues,
Nature's art with every muse.

Mountains rise in regal grace,
Whispering secrets, time can't trace.
Rivers flow like silver threads,
Binding stories that nature spreads.

Birds take flight on painted skies,
Color dances, never lies.
Every shade a story told,
In the twilight, bold and gold.

Stars will shimmer, whispers soft,
As day dips low, the night lifts off.
In this gallery of the divine,
We glimpse the wonder, so sublime.

Enchanted Realms in Astral Light

Beyond the veil of earthly sight,
Lie realms aglow with astral light.
Dreams take shape in shimmering glow,
In these lands where magic flows.

Waves of color swirl and weave,
In patterns that the heart believes.
Voices echo, soft and clear,
Calling forth the ones held dear.

Crystals glisten, casting spells,
With whispers that the silence tells.
In this haven, free from strife,
We dance with shadows, breathe in life.

Stars like lanterns guide the way,
In this enchanted, timeless play.
Every heartbeat tells a tale,
Of wonderment that shall not pale.

Heartstrings Tugged by Celestial Winds

With every breeze, the heart can feel,
The pull of stars, a cosmic reel.
Celestial winds in evening's hush,
Draw dreams like petals in a rush.

Galaxies whisper tales of old,
In currents warm and gently bold.
As stardust spirals through the night,
Hope ignites, a thrilling flight.

Tunes of the universe unwind,
Resonance hugs the wandering mind.
In such moments, we are one,
Connected 'neath the vibrant sun.

Let heartstrings play a symphony,
With every note, a memory.
As celestial winds dance and glide,
We find our way, with love as guide.

Milton Keynes UK
Ingram Content Group UK Ltd.
UKHW021928011224
451790UK00005B/74